You Excel Them All

You Excel Them All

Proverbs 31
Daily Devotional Guide

David E. Crosby

DOVE INSPIRATIONAL PRESS
GRETNA 2010

Library of Congress Cataloging-in-Publication Data

Crosby, David E.
You excel them all : Proverbs 31 daily devotional guide / David E. Crosby.
p. cm.
ISBN 978-1-58980-807-2 (hardcover : alk. paper) 1. Bible. O.T. Proverbs XXXI–Devotional literature. I. Title.
BS1465.55.C76 2010
242'.5–dc22
2009053961

Printed in Singapore
Published by Dove Inspirational Press,
an imprint of Pelican Publishing Company, Inc.
1000 Burmaster Street, Gretna, Louisiana 70053

You Excel Them All

God has created us with amazing potential. Scientists tell us that we use less than 10 percent of our brains. I would suggest to you that we are using less than 10 percent of many of God's gifts, including the virtues of love, joy, peace, patience, and self-control.

We exist in space and time as complex creatures who may be viewed from the physical, the mental, and the spiritual perspectives. We are body, soul, and spirit. As with the triune nature of God, these three agree in one. They provide an astonishing mix of properties and potentialities.

Why did God make us so gifted and unique? God wants us to excel. We know this because of the careful instruction concerning how we may experience abundant life, unleashing the potential of our own lives. We know this because the inspired authors of the Bible are continually urging us beyond the status quo to a new plane of living. We know this because of the passion of the apostle Paul for reaching what is ahead. We know this also because we ourselves want to excel. It is built into us. We want to be good at what we do—the best, if we can. We hunger for excellence both in our work and our personal lives.

A model of excellence can be found in Proverbs 31, the sayings of King Lemuel, which constitute the first nine verses of this chapter. They are recorded as the words of the young king's mother to her son. The famous description of the Virtuous Woman is well known as a Mother's Day text, but it is separated from the sayings of King Lemuel by five chapters in the ancient biblical text, the Septuagint. Therefore, it is likely not part of the sayings of King Lemuel and should stand alone as an anonymous Hebrew acrostic—a poem that goes through the letters of the alphabet with each verse.

The woman of virtue is praiseworthy (NASB): "You excel them all." The NIV translates the sentence, "You surpass them all." We have in the inspired text that follows this declaration a rather detailed description of a person of excellence.

We are going to start with the first words of King Lemuel and move toward the famous text. We will discover actions of body, soul, and spirit that characterize and create excellence in human beings. They are true for both men and women, old and young, rich and poor. They apply across the board because they summarize the aspirations of God for the creatures that are the capstone of his creation.

Day 1

The sayings of King Lemuel—an oracle his mother taught him. Proverbs 31:1

My mother is a powerful woman. She stands only five feet tall, but she is pure energy and dynamite. Everyone has a biological mother. Most of the time, she is a very special person to her child.

Kings have mothers who teach them when they are young. Mothers may or may not know the destiny of their sons and daughters. Some have unknowingly trained kings, and some have done it on purpose.

My mother trained us on purpose. She taught us that we were royalty—sons and daughters of God—so expected great things from us. She warned us of pitfalls and commended to us paths that lead to peace.

I was reading the work of a famous theologian recently. He said that he thought of Jesus as his friend. He learned this, he said, when he was a boy and his favorite song was "What a Friend We Have in Jesus." My immediate thought was this: here is a man who has studied the Bible and theology for fifty years and when he summarizes his faith, he goes back to his boyhood. It reminded me that the things we learn when we are young cast the longest shadows in our lives. When you change the trajectory at the very beginning of a journey, you cause enormous change in the end result.

That's one reason the instruction of our mothers and fathers is so important. They are setting patterns, good or bad, that have tremendous staying power and long effect.

Parents and grandparents are well advised to remind themselves daily of this truth. "As the twig is bent so grows the tree," a proverb observes. We are bending the twigs when we talk and walk and play with our children and grandchildren. Let's bathe every moment with them in prayer. Let's clothe our words in love. Let's remember that we are training royalty—sons and daughters of God.

Scripture Reading: Proverbs 1 and Hebrews 12:1-13

Prayer: Bless my time with the little ones. Help me point them toward you.

Day 2

Oh my son, O son of my womb, O son of my vows. Proverbs 31:2

A mother experiences her child in a way that is surely inaccessible to men and even fathers. She carried the child as a living presence for nine months. The child grows in her womb and comes from her body. Lemuel's mother reminds him of this very special relationship as she instructs him. She wants Lemuel to realize that she has only his best interest at heart. She is seeking to protect him and nurture him with words even as she protected and nurtured him physically when he was in her womb.

The world has learned that stem cells float in the amniotic fluid of the womb. These free-floating stem cells have been used therapeutically and demonstrate the same versatility that embryonic stem cells exhibit. This is important news because routine medical procedures already being practiced can provide stem cells for research and healing without threatening the life in the womb or requiring the destruction of human embryos. The womb is simply full of life. The developing baby floats in a sea of protective fluid with tiny bits of living tissue all around. What an amazing discovery this is! Scientists will spend years just getting a grasp on the healing potential in the womb.

Lemuel is the "son of my vows," his mother says. This means that he is the answer to her prayers. She made promises to the Lord in connection with her son.

Janet is my wife and the mother of our three children. Always, when I hear her pray I am reminded again of how central her children are to her heart and life. Parents should make their children always the object of their prayers.

Scripture Reading: Proverbs 2

Prayer: Thank you, God, for giving us mothers and fathers who love us and pray for us and seek to steer us away from danger and toward the good and true. Help me be such a parent, grandparent, and friend.

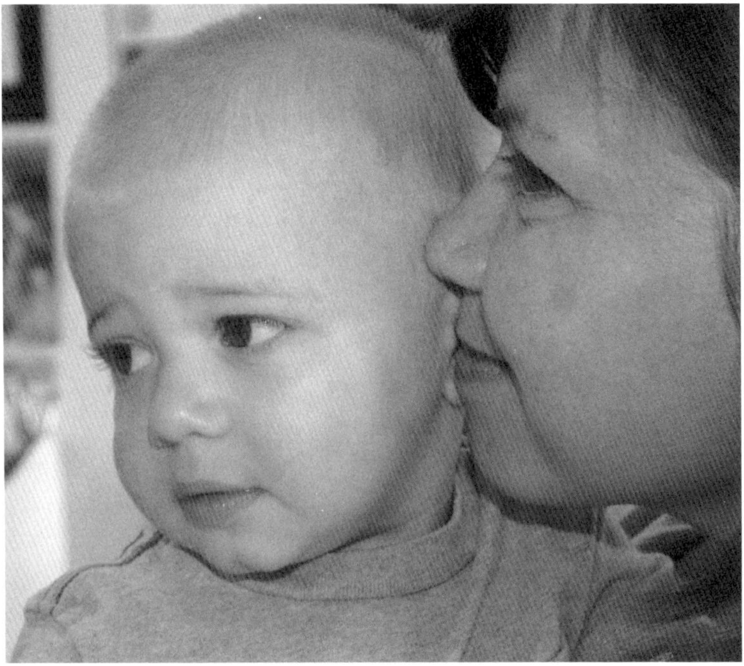

Day 3

Do not spend your strength on women, your vigor on those who ruin kings.
Proverbs 31:3

The king's mother is concerned about his relationship with women. She has reason for concern given the pathetic chronicle of Israelite kings and their affairs and multiple wives. Whenever I think that our society is going down the tubes, a little reading from the Old Testament makes me feel better. What a mess they were—just like us!

The interesting nuance in this mother's warning is the phrase "do not spend your strength" and then "your vigor." Apparently, this mother feels that the power of a king is dissipated by sexual dalliances.

I think that former president William Clinton would probably agree with this mother and has often wished that he would have chosen a different course in his relationship with Monica Lewinsky. In the end, that sickening sexual liaison was a great drain on the leader of our nation, a terrible burden and a crippling distraction to the duties of governance. He spent his strength in a ruinous way.

The high and mighty have ample opportunity to exploit others to satisfy their own desires. It is an ancient story with many illustrations. They keep following this pattern, despite the warnings, because power is intoxicating and sexual desire is compelling.

I was astonished to read the opinion of Dr. James Dobson in regard to the sexual affairs of men. The main reason that men are unfaithful to their wives is "ego needs," Dobson asserts. This is true of both paupers and kings, I suppose. We are all trying to establish our power and presence. Sexual exploits may make us feel like conquerors, but the feeling is an illusion, as President Clinton would certainly testify.

Do not underestimate your own vulnerability to sexual sin. We are all thoroughly and conclusively sexual beings. Our maleness or femaleness is intrinsic to our identity and inseparable from who we are. The power of sex is well attested. Therefore, we must be on our guard, as this mother suggests. If we are to glorify God with our bodies, then we will remain faithful to our spouses and faithful to the God who made us in this key area of love and life.

Scripture Reading: Proverbs 3

Prayer: Dear God, thank you for the gift of sexuality. Thank you for sexual expression within marriage vows. Guard my heart and mind. Give me wisdom and insight so that I remain true to my vows and true to you.

Day 4

It is not for kings, O Lemuel—it is not for kings to drink wine, not for rulers to crave beer. Proverbs 31:4

I was in the grocery store during the Christmas holidays and saw some eggnog that was being distributed by the glass to patrons of the store by a kindly elderly lady.

"Does this have alcohol in it?" I asked. She seemed a little confused by the question, not realizing that my mother has perfected the art of making great eggnog without alcohol.

"Yes, I believe it does," she said. "Is that a problem?"

Well, it's not a problem really, but I passed up the eggnog. I grew up in the home of a teetotaler, and I myself have been one my whole life. I don't drink alcohol. When I think about the reason, I think about my father and mother and their insistence that "nothing good ever came out of that bottle."

Despite the protests of some exegetes, I suspect that Jesus drank fermented wine. I don't have any other explanation for his enemies calling him a drunkard and his admission that he came "eating and drinking" (see Luke 7:33-34). And I doubt that in a hot climate without refrigeration they could effectively prevent grape juice from turning into wine.

I can present a theological justification for refusing all alcohol and have done so elsewhere. But what I would like to note instead is the strange insistence of this mother that it is "not for kings to drink." The feasting of kings is legendary. Their tables are always spilling over with wine. When you have finally "made it," you can afford the expensive beverages that make you feel better. We actually associate power and money with alcohol.

Not this mom. She wants her royal son to stay away from the stuff. She wants him to envision his place at the head of the table without a glass of wine or a mug of beer. She will not hear her son's retort, "Everyone is doing it!"

"You know better than that, Lemuel. Not everyone is doing it.

And you are not 'everyone.' You, my son, are a king, and kings must behave differently."

Scripture Reading: Proverbs 4

Prayer: Dear Lord, help me to see myself seated in heavenly places in Christ Jesus. Give me a picture of myself in the place of power and influence without any need for the deadening impact of alcohol on my mind or my heart.

Day 5

Lest they drink and forget what the law decrees, and deprive all the oppressed of their rights. Proverbs 31:5

Here's the real problem with alcohol: it may be used to anesthetize the king.

The responsibilities of governing weigh heavy on the soul. Sometimes the prince wants to be king so that, when he himself sits upon the throne, he will no longer have to listen to the orders of another. He wants to be king so that he can escape the responsibilities of daily life.

People escape in various ways. Some disappear into sports, some into work, some into romance novels, and some into drugs. None of these is intrinsically evil. God made work and romance, hunger and exercise. But when the person with influence and authority runs away from the real world and into the play world, the poor are neglected and the oppressed are forgotten.

The law of God is clear—kings and societies will be judged, not by how they treat the powerful but by how they treat the powerless. The treatment of the widows and orphans tells us more about justice and truth in any regime than the treatment of the rich and powerful.

When a person in a position of authority is inclined to escape the demands of the office, the ones who suffer are those who can neither defend themselves nor speak for themselves. Lemuel's mother feels very deeply that the poor have rights. They can be deprived of those rights by an irresponsible or inattentive government. Therefore, Lemuel must see himself as champion of the poor and oppressed when he ascends to the throne. And so must all who follow Christ Jesus.

When Jesus comes, the poor get good news. When Christians come into authority, it should always be good news for the poor and oppressed. This truth may feel uncomfortable to us, but it has the weight of holy writ and we should not seek to escape it.

Scripture Reading: Proverbs 5

Prayer: Gracious Father, teach me how to emulate you when I deal with the poor and oppressed. Give me a heart for those who are in trouble. Show me how to use my wealth and position to ease their pain and give them hope.

Day 6

Give beer to those who are perishing, wine to those who are in anguish.
Proverbs 31:6

Now here is an interesting text. Someone pointed this out to me recently, knowing that I did not drink alcohol.

"What do you do with that?" she asked.

My first response is to insist that my practice is my own. It is not based on a proof text though I think Proverbs 23:29-35 is a pretty good one. You might want to stop and read it.

Secondly, I know that godly people in all generations have taken the approach of moderation rather than total abstinence. I am not interested in insisting that total abstinence is the right approach in all times and cultures and for all people everywhere.

Thirdly, some people do have reason to deaden their feelings. I think this is what Lemuel's mother was pointing to. Some people do need anesthesia. They are dying or they are in anguish. We do well to relieve their pain. The best anesthesia available for the ancients was alcoholic beverages.

Lemuel's mother is presenting a different perspective on wealth and drinking. She is saying that the wealthier and more powerful we get, the less we can afford to imbibe. The curiosity of this position is that it turns our own ideas inside out. Ultimately, wealth and power do not free us; they restrict us. They place more demands on us.

Jesus said, "From everyone who has been given much, much will be demanded; and from the one who has been entrusted with much, much more will be asked" (Luke 12:48).

This is an economic principle that we are all familiar with. We judge ourselves treated fairly when we receive a raise in compensation as part of increased responsibility. We are aiming high—and we should. But when we get there, we should not think that we will be even freer to do whatever we want. Lock the beverage closet. Once we have arrived, our responsibilities will require even greater sobriety.

Scripture Reading: Proverbs 6

Prayer: Dear Lord Jesus, I have been given so much. I need your Holy Spirit today, helping me to be wise and fair in all I do.

Day 7

Give beer to those who are perishing, wine to those who are in anguish; let them drink and forget their poverty and remember their misery no more. Proverbs 31:6-7

Verses 6 and 7 have to be considered together. This is a good example of how the context must be taken into account when interpreting Scripture.

Lemuel's mother appears to be suggesting that the poor and oppressed need a good, stiff shot to feel better. They need to forget and remember no more. But this would be drunkenness, and the Bible consistently condemns drunkenness. It is in a lot of lists (e.g. Romans 13:13) of things to avoid.

Here is my understanding of these two verses—they are hyperbole, overstatement for effect. Jesus used this tool often, following the example of many great teachers.

Misery and poverty, anguish and dying—these are the circumstances of many people in the world. And they are circumstances that can drive people to drink. We may not agree with their preferred route of escape, but we can see how they would want to get out of their pain if only for a little while.

But they are not the circumstances of young Lemuel. He is healthy and rich and powerful. His future lies before him like a grand assignment. His mother insists that he has no cause to escape into a bottle. In fact, he goes against his divine and human responsibilities to do so.

I chatted with a twelve-year-old girl who told me of her grand dreams. Then she said goodbye, walked down a dusty path, and went back into the mud hut in the impoverished barrio in Colombia that she called home. I shook my head as she walked away, and I wished that I could wave a wand and change her future. The greatest poverty of the poor is that they grow up to live in a world without dreams.

Scripture Reading: Proverbs 7

Prayer: Give me the opportunity, Lord, to lift somebody today, to give them a hand up from their discouragement and a way out of their despair.

Day 8

Speak up for those who cannot speak for themselves, for the rights of all who are destitute. Proverbs 31:8

Speech is powerful. Often part of "doing something" is saying something. Often saying something changes things dramatically and gets us in a lot of hot water. It takes courage to speak the truth to powerful people.

You would think that a king could easily say anything he wanted to say. Not so. Powerful people, like the rest of us, must consider the effects of their words. Their words may have resounding impact not only in their own countries and on their own people, but worldwide. Kings are surrounded by powerful people. Their peers are other heads of state. They meet to discuss military action, economic alliances, and border disputes. We probably agree that kings must watch their words more carefully than ordinary people. Perhaps now, more than ever before, careless words play havoc among the nations. Stock markets around the world respond immediately to the predictions and suggestions of kings and presidents. Verbal miscues by influential people roar like wildfires through the internet blogs.

Lemuel's mother has some advice for him in regard to his speech: "Speak up for those who cannot speak for themselves." Who is this woman? She has the gall to say this to the king? Oh, she is his mother. He knows she only wants what is best for him. In her position, she can speak the truth without fear. This is a mother's privilege.

Lemuel's mother does speak God's truth. Lemuel the king needs to worry about his words, not so much in regard to the powerful, but in regard to the powerless. According to the Bible, governments are judged not by how they treat the squeaky wheels, but by how they treat those who have no voice.

We have a speaking assignment. As persons of excellence, we will speak for those at work and school who are powerless and cannot speak for themselves. As we do this, we will express the love of Christ and offer sound counsel to people in power.

Scripture Reading: Proverbs 8

Prayer: Dear God, give me the wisdom to defend the oppressed where my life intersects with theirs. Give me the words to speak to those in authority that will bring justice and hope to the needy. Help me find my voice and bring you glory.

Day 9

Speak up and judge fairly; defend the rights of the poor and needy.
Proverbs 31:9

The poor and needy have rights. They should enjoy equal access to justice; they should expect to be treated fairly in the courts of the land. This is a repeated theme in Scripture. God has an intense hatred for injustice, bribes, and weighted scales that allow the rich to prey upon the poor.

In my own hometown of New Orleans the crime rate has been driven to astronomical levels. Turf wars and drug lords spur homicides. Usual social conditions that constrain crime, such as neighbors walking at night and good lighting in public places, no longer pertain in our devastated city. Two of our ministers at First Baptist have been victims of crime since Hurricane Katrina. One came home from a trip to find his house robbed and vandalized. Home invasions have become far too common, especially in the flood zone where so many houses still sit empty.

Citizens can do some things about these matters, but keeping the peace is the responsibility of government. Lemuel's mother is correct to call upon the young king to "judge fairly." Nothing deters crime as effectively as the certainty of judgment.

In New Orleans, where crime is at historically high levels, the security of the evidence room for the police department is under review. The flood waters of Hurricane Katrina churned its contents into muddy soup. Management of the room now seems under perpetual investigation. Confiscated cash has disappeared. The integrity of the crime-fighting process is in question.

One man was arrested in the chaos after the storm and jailed for fourteen months without being charged with a crime. He could not speak English and simply got lost in the system. When the guilty go free and the rights of the poor are neglected, the righteous suffer.

An effective and fair criminal justice system is a requirement for peace and safety in all societies. Those who establish and repair such systems are doing God's work.

Scripture Reading: Proverbs 9

Prayer: Thank you, God, for being holy and just and for ordering your universe on those terms. Help me to be fair and just in all my dealings with others. And help me to do all I can to make sure that my community is just and fair to all its citizens.

Day 10

A wife of noble character who can find? She is worth far more than rubies. Proverbs 31:10

Proverbs 31:10 begins an acrostic poem about a woman of strength and courage. These twenty-two verses describe her life and demeanor in some detail. This may be the longest description of a single person's character in the Bible.

The Hebrew word *chayil,* translated "noble character," means "strength, might, valor, or substance." It is usually used in the Old Testament to refer to the strength of an army or fighting man. We make a mistake to relegate the passage of the Virtuous Woman and her noble character to Mother's Day sermons, for the person described in this text displays qualities of character that every human being should strive to possess.

The woman described is also a wife, and this relationship may be what enables the author to describe her so thoroughly. In the intimate bonds of marriage we learn the true constitution of a person's inner being.

The marriage relationship is tremendously rewarding and demanding. To marry a person of true nobility, courage, and virtue is to receive one of life's great gifts. The rarity of this type of individual is the author's first point. Rubies, to which the noble woman is compared, were some of the rarest and most precious stones in the ancient world. A spouse of this caliber is both rare and valuable beyond description. Noble character as he will describe it is surely the exception rather than the rule.

If the writer is Solomon, as many people think, then his experience with women is very broad. Solomon had 700 wives and 300 concubines, and his wives turned his heart away from the Lord (see 1 Kings 11:1-4). Solomon was not wise, it appears, when dealing with women. This poem could be his wish list, his dream wife, written in hindsight and describing the woman he never found.

Scripture Reading: Proverbs 10

Prayer: *Dear God, make me a virtuous spouse to the one I love. Build in me courage and strength. Help me to bring to my marriage this quality of character so that I may be a blessing to my family and all about me.*

Day 11

Her husband has full confidence in her and lacks nothing of value.
Proverbs 31:11

Full confidence in someone—that is another rarity. The wife is full of virtue and the husband is full of confidence.

The Hebrew text contains the little word *leb,* or "heart." The King James Version keeps this and says, "The heart of her husband doth safely trust in her." I think this translation adds an important nuance to the meaning. Down deep inside, in his heart of hearts, this man fully trusts his wife.

The word for "husband" may be surprising. It is *ba'al,* from which we get Baal (you remember the gods of Baal). It is the word for owner or "lord," and it expresses the authority over and even ownership of the wife that belonged to the husband in that ancient society. Despite the legal arrangements of any particular society, no husband is safe who cannot trust his wife and vice versa. Mutual trust is absolutely essential for security and peace in the marriage and family. Thus, this woman of noble character is one in whom the husband can safely trust. She will not use him or manipulate him or deceive him or betray him. She is absolutely reliable in every way.

This is a goal toward which every man and woman can move. Christ, our bedrock, is supremely trustworthy and is building in us this kind of character. We are all in process, but we can move deliberately toward the day when others will confidently say, "Now there is a spouse who is fully trustworthy in every way."

The wife of noble character is more valuable than rubies and her trusting husband lacks nothing of value. He is wealthy beyond words for he has a spouse who is strong, loving, and faithful.

Scripture Reading: Proverbs 11

Prayer: Dear Lord, thank you for the inestimable value of those near me who are trustworthy. Thank you for placing such virtuous people in my life. Help me to be one of them today.

Day 12

She brings him good, not harm, all the days of her life. Proverbs 31:12

This godly wife does not harm her husband. She does him good always. The words for "good" and "harm" are used hundreds of times in the Old Testament. Usually they are translated "good" and "evil." These same words are used in the name for the "tree of the knowledge of good and evil" in Genesis 2:9. Adam and Eve had a terrible time with that tree. They both ended up doing evil by eating its fruit. Neither of them did good for the other. But this amazing woman of virtue will not follow the path of Eve. She will resist the evil and perform the good toward her husband.

As fundamental as this sounds, I am amazed at how often spouses do not follow this course. Instead of kindness, they choose pettiness. Instead of patience, they choose aggravation. Instead of self-control, they choose excess. While it seems that simple kindness would be easy to display consistently toward the spouse of your vows, that is not the case. Married people are often unkind toward one another.

Proverbs 31:10 is an introduction to the Virtuous Woman. Verse 11, the second verse of the poem, describes the effect of her virtue upon the most important person in her life. This third verse stands as the summary of her character. Concerning her husband—and all others—she does good, not harm, every day and all the days of her life.

When an inquirer described Jesus as "good teacher," Jesus objected and said, "Why do you call me good? No one is good—except God alone" (Luke 18:18-19). We know that Jesus was exceptionally good. The point he was making with the young man is that only God is truly and thoroughly good and that the young man's assumption of his own goodness was in error. He was also saying that to be good is to be like God.

Scripture Reading: Proverbs 12

Prayer: Good Teacher, show me how to emulate you in my dealings with others. Discipline my mouth so that my words are good. Guide my actions so that I do good toward the ones I love. And shape my thoughts so that I am planning good rather than scheming with evil intent.

Day 13

She selects wool and flax and works with eager hands. Proverbs 31:13

I lived on a farm and worked for ranchers when I was a boy. When we sheared the goats and sheep, we always separated the kid and lamb hair from the rest. It would bring so seven dollars per pound where the adult hair was only worth three dollars. As a boy, I wondered about this distinction so I ran my fingers through the mohair of an adult Angora goat and then felt the hair of a kid. The difference is undeniable. If you took the time to really look and feel, you would always prefer the kid hair to the adult. It is finer, softer, and brighter in color.

The woman of virtue is in the business of selecting just the right materials for her work. She is looking intently for the lamb's wool, the kid hair. She takes the time to identify and select the best available. She experiences longing, delight, and pleasure as she takes the wool and flax into her hands. This is no humdrum, boring drudgery for her. She is motivated by love and kindness in her work. She wants her children and husband to know the pleasant feel of the softest wool rather than the harsh scratch of the stiff strands.

She is distinguished as much by her attitude and motivation as she is by the care in her process. All of us know how it feels to be the recipient of someone's hasty work done half as well as it could have been. We know how it feels to receive a work of duty and obligation without the tender touch of love and delight.

Excellence involves both craftsmanship and longing. It is a combination of the desire to do things well and a deep love for the recipient of our work.

Scripture Reading: Proverbs 13

Prayer: Dear Lord Jesus, I have a list of tasks before me today, but I do not want to march through them bored and detached. Give me the grace to do my best even in the simple things. Help me bless those who will be touched by the work I do today.

Day 14

She is like the merchant ships, bringing her food from afar. Proverbs 31:14

Ships come by the thousands from all over the world to the Port of New Orleans. They bring the steel that will go upriver to Detroit and the oil that will go to the coastal refineries, among many other things. They are a sight to see, those great ships, as they navigate the river's crescent. They represent the economic engine of our region and the international trade that makes the financial world go 'round.

The woman of virtue is like one of those ships. She is the vehicle through which her household receives the best supplies for the smokehouse, the oven, and the kitchen table. The daily task of feeding the family does not weigh her down. She goes to great lengths to make certain that her responsibilities result in the best possible product. She is not insulted to be the cargo-bearer for the family. She is blessed.

As I read about this woman, I think about her husband and children. They had better notice her good work; they had better be grateful! No one should work this hard at doing the very best and go unappreciated. I think, however, that she is often just that: unappreciated. Children sit down at the table and devour their food and drink and never think about how heavy those bags and bottles were when pulled from the shelf, plopped into the cart, heaved into the SUV, slid into the pantry, and then lifted to the countertop. If she is doing this in order that she might receive praise from her kids, she is going to be disappointed.

But praise is not her purpose. She loves them and will do her best whether they notice or not. That is part of excellence.

Scripture Reading: Proverbs 14

Prayer: Dear God, you have done all the heavy lifting in my relationship with you. You loved me before I could understand love. You cared for me when I cared nothing for you. Teach me how to behave today in ways that emulate your self-giving love.

Day 15

She gets up while it is still dark; she provides food for her family and portions for her servant girls. Proverbs 31:15

I never appreciated the work of my mother until I became an adult. Now I am amazed every time I think about her caring for thirteen children, all just as oblivious to the load she carried as I was. I can remember the sounds in the kitchen each morning, the rattling of dishes and the opening and closing of cupboards. I remember the smells that wafted into my bedroom before my feet hit the floor. My mother was up working on breakfast. Dad might have gone to work already, but all the kids were still in bed. When did this woman sleep? I wonder now. She was still working when I went to bed and up before dawn day after day and year after year. Even now she comes to family reunions with pans of rolls rising during the drive.

Children are usually unaware of all the sacrifices made for them. Their amazement blossoms later. However, the adult who writes the poem in Proverbs 31 appreciates the hard work of the woman of the house. He knows the demands that are upon her, and he admires her for the hours she puts in caring for her family and servants.

Like children, husbands are not always appreciative of their wives. They are often slow to learn how to clean up their own messes, let alone the messes the children make. This lack of sensitivity to the endless household chores should be corrected earlier rather than later—for the sake of everyone in the house.

A person of excellence puts in a full day's work. He or she is not waiting around for someone to prod them into action. Excellence takes the initiative and acts upon the obvious.

Scripture Reading: Proverbs 15

Prayer: Thank you, Lord, for acting to save me when I was oblivious to my need. Thank you for loving me when I had no capacity to love you. Help me to be willing to care for those who are sometimes oblivious and sometimes incapacitated by forces beyond their control. Give me strength to do my work today knowing that I answer to you for every day in every way.

Day 16

She considers a field and buys it; out of her earnings she plants a vineyard. Proverbs 31:16

Now here we have an interesting notation concerning the character of a virtuous woman. She is an entrepreneur! We would not have expected this brush stroke in the portrait, especially from an ancient writer in a patriarchal society. Even supposing that she is using the name and authority of her husband, it is still remarkable that she travels and works in this part of her world, initiating real estate transactions and developing agricultural assets.

It is difficult to find such women anywhere else in the Bible. Abigail is the single one who comes to mind, and she was pressed into the roll because her husband was such a fool (read her remarkable story in 1 Samuel 25).

Excellence is not simply about honesty, integrity, and hard work, although these are indispensable. Excellence also includes financial savvy and good stewardship of our possessions. Any real estate transaction involves risk, and this woman surely experienced setbacks if she negotiated real estate deals regularly. Planting vineyards is likewise a business of some risk. Who knows what the weather will bring?

We do not achieve excellence in this life by ordering our world according to fear of financial ruin. She has confidence that God will guide her as she manages her family's earthly wealth. She also believes that seedtime and harvest will continue to come to her world just as God promised in his words to Noah (Genesis 8:22). Her faith in God extends to the natural cycles of the earth.

Some people are refugees, members of persecuted minorities, and subjects of despotic regimes. They live in such turbulent political environs that they cannot count on reaping where they sow. Most of us, however, fulfill God's plan by tilling and tending the earth, investing wisely in the economy of our time, and trusting that God will care for us if disaster comes.

Scripture Reading: Proverbs 16

Prayer: Lord Jesus, I ask for wisdom in my financial affairs. Help me to invest my money wisely and to manage properly what I own. Give me a good harvest from the work of my hands so that I can be generous with those around me who are in need.

Day 17

She sets about her work vigorously; her arms are strong for her tasks.
Proverbs 31:17

The energy of this woman is truly remarkable. She is here and there and everywhere, buying and planting and transporting goods.

Excellence in living includes a good attitude toward our work. On the whole, we should be eager to work. Even though Adam was cursed with making a living "by the sweat of your brow" (Genesis 3:19), work itself is to be accomplished each day under the scrutiny of God as if he were the true employer (see Colossians 3:23).

Two different words for "strength" are used in this verse to describe the woman of virtue. The first, "vigorously," is all about personal and physical strength. This woman is active and fit. The Bible instructs us to care for our bodies; we are to treat them as the temple of the living God (see 1 Corinthians 6:19).

Nevertheless, we should not equate physical fitness with godliness. God specializes in using the weak and infirm to confound the healthy and strong. But we should be developing and maintaining healthy exercise and eating habits. These disciplines will usually extend our usefulness to God and others. Sometimes we cannot go the second mile because we are not in good enough shape to do so!

The second word for strength here is all about persistence, boldness, and assurance. Excellence in living includes these qualities of character.

The recovery work that we are engaged in here in New Orleans and the surrounding region is sometimes overwhelming. The extent of the damage from the flood that inundated the city on August 29, 2005, is hard to describe. Not only are thousands of structures still blighted and abandoned, but thousands of people still struggle daily with the sorrow and grief brought on by the great storm. But the flood zone is a great place for persistence, boldness, and assurance. When we interact with friends and family and gather together at church, we are all looking for encouragement and hope. We often renew our strength as we see and experience the determination and positive attitude of our friends.

Scripture Reading: Proverbs 17

Prayer: Father in Heaven, I do not always feel strong and hopeful. Sometimes I feel weak and exhausted. Renew my strength as I go through this day. Give me a genuine smile and a spring in my step. Thank you for walking beside me and for carrying me when I cannot make it on my own. I give myself to you and plunge into the work.

Day 18

She sees that her trading is profitable, and her lamp does not go out at night. Proverbs 31:18

This sounds like trading on the stock market and it is akin to it. She is buying and selling, looking for bargains, tasting the spice and mint, and making sure of the quality of her goods. This person of excellence looks for excellence in all about her. She does not want to simply make do, she wants to do well. She works to lift her life to the next level in every dimension.

Excellence requires paying attention to details. Some people are detail oriented, but I am not one of them. I have to work at slowing down to notice and care for the details. It behooves me to discipline the pace of my life so that I can follow in the footsteps of this woman.

She is not paralyzed by perpetual analysis, though, and we should not be either. She tastes the flour or salt to make sure it is the best grade and then is decisive in her buying and selling. She couples action with careful attention, a truly profitable combination.

Excellence in living is not achieved as a passing moment of success. The lamp of this woman burns all night. She has enough oil to keep the flame burning. She has true staying power.

We reveal our character both in moments of challenge and through years of persistence. Snapshots can uncover some important things, but they do not tell the whole story. Excellence involves having the determination to remain on course through good times and bad, knowing that the way we behave is ordered by the Lord and is its own reward.

All Christians should take heart that God takes the long view. Failure is not final. Our shortcomings may be overcome by our long endurance. Darkness falls on every man. Just don't let the lamp go out. Keep the oil burning. We have an endless supply through our connection with the Father above.

Scripture Reading: Proverbs 18

Prayer: Holy Spirit of God, I feel sometimes that the night is pressing in around my soul. I am anxious and frightened. Calm my spirit, Lord. Help me to trust in you when things begin to shake. Give me the supply of oil that I need to keep my light burning through the night.

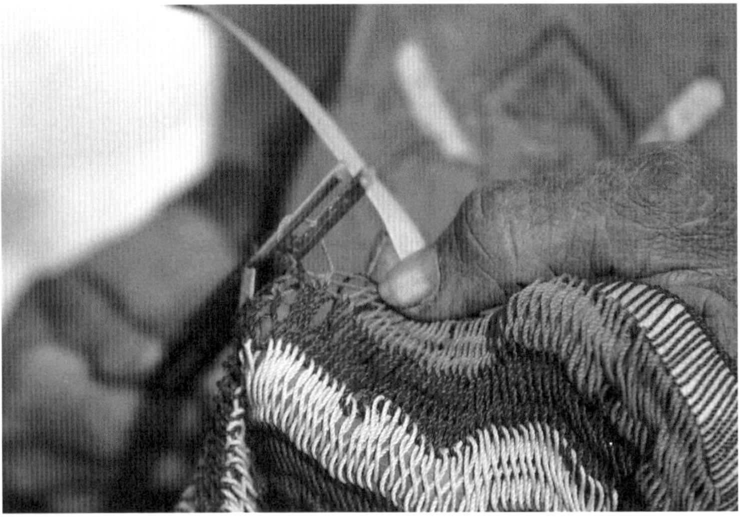

Day 19

In her hand she holds the distaff and grasps the spindle with her fingers.
Proverbs 31:19

This woman's versatility is astonishing. She is buying real estate in the morning and sewing shirts that night. The breadth of her interests and expertise is staggering. Many others have pointed out the broad range of duties that a homemaker embraces. Depending on the division of labor in the household she may be courier and merchant, breadwinner and bread baker, mother and CEO. She has an endless array of possibilities before her.

Excellence may be achieved in almost any combination of tasks. Based upon interests and giftedness, we craft a life that emphasizes our strengths and addresses immediate needs. We focus on what we do best while making sure that the rest gets done.

I see a servant spirit in many of these verses, including this one, where we find the lady of the house making yarn. I doubt that this was a task she relished or one that she alone could do. I suspect that the servant girls could be trained to make yarn and weave garments. Yet, back from a day in the marketplace, she is willing to grip the distaff and go to work. She knows this needs to be done, and she does it. Perhaps she thinks as the distaff spins how she might pass on this chore to others. Or maybe she reserves it for herself alone as a time of meditation and decompression from a hard day's work.

I suspect that this husband never touches the spindle except perhaps to move it or repair it. He sits by the fire as his wife spins, and he contemplates the spirit of a woman who never tires of helping others and never ceases to amaze him.

Scripture Reading: Proverbs 19

Prayer: Dear God, give me a servant spirit today. I know that there is much around the house that needs done. Help me set the pace at cleaning up the common spaces and doing for others in my household as you have done for me.

Day 20

She opens her arms to the poor and extends her hands to the needy.
Proverbs 31:20

Care of the poor is part of excellence in living. It is part of being a virtuous and noble person. This reoccurring theme in both Old and New Testaments is definitive for those who wish to follow Jesus of Nazareth. Note the parallel between "poor" and "needy." The two phrases of this verse reinforce each other and seek to communicate the same thing.

No one wants to be needy—full of needs. Sometimes we characterize a person as being very "needy." We may mean by this that the person needs attention or affirmation continually, that they suffer from insecurities and a poor self-image and must be assured of their good status in the human community. The whole and healthy are tempted to look down on the poor and needy. Those afflicted with deformities discover that they are sometimes shunned. Those who are sick find that old friends are reluctant to come by and see them.

When we see a person who is not quite whole for some reason, we are tempted to blame them for their condition. "If they had lived differently," we may think to ourselves, "they would not be in this situation." Sometimes that thought may be partially true. Lifestyles do put us at risk. However, we are not in a position to judge others. We can all use "I told you so" when people around us get sick or injured. The fact is, all of us get sick and die. It is a universal condition.

We should not be repelled by the needy. As followers of Jesus, we should be rushing to their aid. If we are taken advantage of when we do so—and sometimes that will happen—we should learn greater discernment. But in the end even God Almighty helps people—lots of them—who just grab his gifts and run. To see our loving-kindness poured out on the ground, that is a divine dilemma.

Scripture Reading: Proverbs 20

Prayer: Gracious God, you have been so good to me even when I turned my back and ran from you. Thank you for continuing to love me more than I am capable of loving you. Help me to do the same today for people in my life.

Day 21

When it snows, she has no fear for her household; for all of them are clothed in scarlet. Proverbs 31:21

When it snows in New Orleans, we are all amazed. It actually snowed on Christmas Day, 2004, the Christmas before Hurricane Katrina, and New Orleanians were graced with another beautiful white Christmas just a few years after that, in 2008. We scraped the white stuff into piles, built snowmen, and threw soggy snowballs.

The virtuous are prepared even for such rare eventualities as snow in a warm climate. These occurrences could be emergencies to those who are ill prepared. As in New Orleans, snow is not common in Israel. In fact, I understand that Mount Hermon, the site of the only ski resort in Israel, is the only place that gets snow regularly. If virtue means that a family in Israel is well prepared for snow, then virtue means that a family in New Orleans is well prepared for hurricanes. I am inspired to prepare more thoroughly for storms and evacuations.

The amazing woman in Proverbs is a homemaker, among many other things, and she carries the responsibility for clothing the family properly, with clothes of scarlet ready for the cold weather. Scarlet is a great color for cold and snowy days. The coloring of this ancient cloth also means that it is material of the finest quality. These garments are warm and cozy on those unusual days when they are needed by all family members. She attends to this important matter with such care that even unusual circumstances cause her no fear. She is not afraid of snow; she is ready for it.

We learn here one of the keys to reducing anxiety: good preparation. It is not a cure-all, of course, but it does help to use our energy for practical readiness rather than needless frittering.

Scripture Reading: Proverbs 21

Prayer: Heavenly Father, you alone know the future. You alone know what storms may come to our coast this next hurricane season. I pray for another year without the need to evacuate. But I pray that, should the call come, you will help me and my family be so prepared that we are free to help others in their need.

Photo by Jared Pryer

Day 22

She makes coverings for her bed; she is clothed in fine linen and purple.
Proverbs 31:22

The concern for bed coverings I can appreciate, though not aesthetically. I have no eye for color or matching patterns or compatibility between comforter and curtains. These things usually escape me though I can see such attention to detail if I slow down enough to notice.

What I can immediately appreciate about bed coverings is their warmth. I enjoy a good blanket on a cold night. When I was a boy living in the frigid environs of northern Minnesota, I woke up often to the sound of the radiator popping as the water in the heating system began to warm and circulate. Oil was expensive even back in 1960, so my father cut off the furnace almost every night. My morning routine was to jump out of bed, grab my clothes for the day and lay them on the radiator, then jump back under the covers until the clothes warmed up.

Part of excellence in living is paying attention to the concerns that bless others. Frankly, I never thought about where my quilts came from or how they got on my bed. My mother, bless her heart, thought of these things for me and my siblings. It was a joy and delight for her to do so even though she knew how mindless we all were.

The person of virtue is also attentive to her own appearance. She is not ostentatious, but she dresses appropriately as the manager of her household and the spouse of a city elder. Her husband is proud of her in every way. I believe he knows he has married a woman of rare value, but he receives his amazing spouse daily as one of God's chief gifts to him, and he enjoys every minute of her blessings and attention.

Scripture Reading: Proverbs 22

Prayer: Dear God, I am blessed everyday by the kindnesses of those I love. Help me to recognize their acts of service, to see their devotion to my need, and to respond in kind. Keep me from the stinginess of heart that withholds love until it is given. Help me be more like you—focused upon the needs of others, anticipating those needs even before they ask for help.

Day 23

Her husband is respected at the city gate, where he takes his seat among the elders of the land. Proverbs 31:23

This husband sits in a coveted chair. He takes his seat in the community with an assured presence and an appropriate self-confidence. He does not take his position for granted; he earns it every day by wise judgment and honest administration.

Here is a husband, however, whose position of respect is in large measure connected to the woman he has married—and he knows it. Not only does he have a respected position, but he has a spouse who enhances him and his work in every way. Some of the elders who sit with him are objects of pity because they have not married well. Some are objects of scorn because they have shown such poor judgment in domestic matters.

This husband has learned the enhancement that healthy relationships can bring to his life. He treasures his wife as a friend and soul mate. He defines his own health, progress, and significance in terms of this key relationship. Think of this husband's position. He has security that runs deeper than any financial or business standing. This bedrock security comes through his marriage. He has full confidence in his wife; therefore, he lacks nothing of value that life can deliver to him. He would far prefer financial destitution to being a widower. He can envision himself without political clout or authority, but he cannot see himself without his wife. He would trade every valuable thing he owns to preserve his marriage.

Think of the years of honest labor, earnest conversation, and ready self-sacrifice that these two persons have conferred upon one another. The strength of virtue is its staying power. Here we have an end product that cannot be purchased with money—only with faithful love.

Scripture Reading: Proverbs 23

Prayer: Dear God, you have been so good to me in the relationships you have given me. Thank you for family members and friends who love me and care for me. Help me to be the leader in serving my family and friends. Show me all the ways in which I can be a blessing. And help me, in the midst of my serving, to attend to my own needs as well.

Day 24

She makes linen garments and sells them, and supplies the merchants with sashes. Proverbs 31:24

Virtue is not the work of a moment or a minute. It is the work of a lifetime. We cannot take "virtue pills" to immediately change our character. We cannot count on instant changes to our inner being. Instead, those who strive for excellence take on a task that does not end this side of heaven.

Excellence is the effort to conform our behavior and being to the character of God himself. God alone is perfect, but we have great potential to be like him—more like him than we are today. We do not finally arrive at a destination on this journey to excellence. We continually strive toward the goal, but we do not apprehend it: "Not that I have already obtained all this, or have already been made perfect, but I press on to take hold of that for which Christ Jesus took hold of me. Brothers, I do not consider myself yet to have taken hold of it" (Philippians 3:12-13).

The woman of excellence seems tireless, full of energy, and abounding in ideas and activities. Yet I know that she is weary when she lays her head down at night. She has aches and pains as do we all. She experiences disappointments with her children and her husband. She is frustrated sometimes, and sometimes she grapples with despair. No human being flies through life oblivious to these emotions and challenges. The greatest battle we fight is the inner battle to maintain our spiritual equilibrium when life surprises us with terrible trouble.

Scripture Reading: Proverbs 24

Prayer: Father in Heaven, you know every battle that I fight. You have equipped me spiritually to live in victory each day. I want to be more than a conqueror today. Give me hope and faith as I deal with people. Help me to be bold in my witness for you. May I have the chance today to lift up the fallen and care for the needy.

Day 25

She is clothed with strength and dignity; she can laugh at the days to come. Proverbs 31:25

I enjoy seeing this godly woman laughing. The New American Standard Bible translates the phrase, "She smiles at the future." The King James version reads, "She shall rejoice in time to come." This laugh of hers I imagine to be infectious. When asked about the future—tomorrow or next year—her head goes back a little and she laughs and smiles. She is at peace with the future, as she is the past. She lives in the moment and is not threatened by what lies behind or ahead.

The future is not ominous to this woman of virtue. It is not foreboding or dark. Her ability to smile at the future is a true sign of faith and trust in God. She knows that the Almighty Lord of glory holds the future in his hands, and she can trust him with it.

Every morning she puts on her clothing of strength and virtue. She will work that day from before dawn until after dark. She will speak and behave in ways that are consistent with her faith in God. She will not compromise her integrity. And when each day is through—and she is tired from her work—she gives herself and her family and all that she has to the Lord who owns her soul.

She has children and maybe grandchildren. She has financial holdings. If she chose to do so, she could fret about the days ahead. She chooses not to do so. She sleeps soundly. She knows what is in her purview to change, and she knows what is out of her hands. And she smiles when she thinks of tomorrow.

Scripture Reading: Proverbs 25

Prayer: Dear Lord, I want to be clothed today with strength and dignity. Give me the energy and determination that I need, and help me to honor you with my choices. I trust you completely with myself and all that belongs to me. Help me to work and live in peace.

Day 26

She speaks with wisdom, and faithful instruction is on her tongue.
Proverbs 31:26

Faithfulness is a key dimension of excellence in living. This person of virtue has confidence in the future in part because she inspires the confidence of her family and friends. They know they can trust her to do what she believes is best for all involved in any situation. She is faithful.

Faithfulness begins in our relationship with God. If we love him, then we want to be like him. And he is perfectly faithful. His faithfulness, in fact, "continues through all generations" (Psalm 100:5). To be faithful is to be like God.

The faithful instruction mentioned in this verse is an instruction that is faithful to both the word of God and to the hearer. It does not invent its own course but holds to the teachings of Scripture and the character of God. It is not selfish. It does not pursue a hidden agenda, nor is it a mask for using another person. The person of virtue does not treat others as a means to an end. She treats them with the dignity they deserve as creatures of infinite worth in the sight of God.

Faithful instruction always is good for the hearer, even when it is hard to receive. "Faithful are the wounds of a friend," says Proverbs 27:6. The words of the virtuous are covered with love. Love for the other person is her chief motivation as she gives them instruction.

Choose your counselors wisely. Seek the wisdom of those who have demonstrated their love for you and for God and whose lives line up with what you know is right.

Scripture Reading: Proverbs 26

Prayer: Lord God, help me to be a wise counselor today for those around me. Help my words to be faithful to them and to you. Bring the Scripture to my mind as I go through my day, and may my words and deeds be faithful to your teachings.

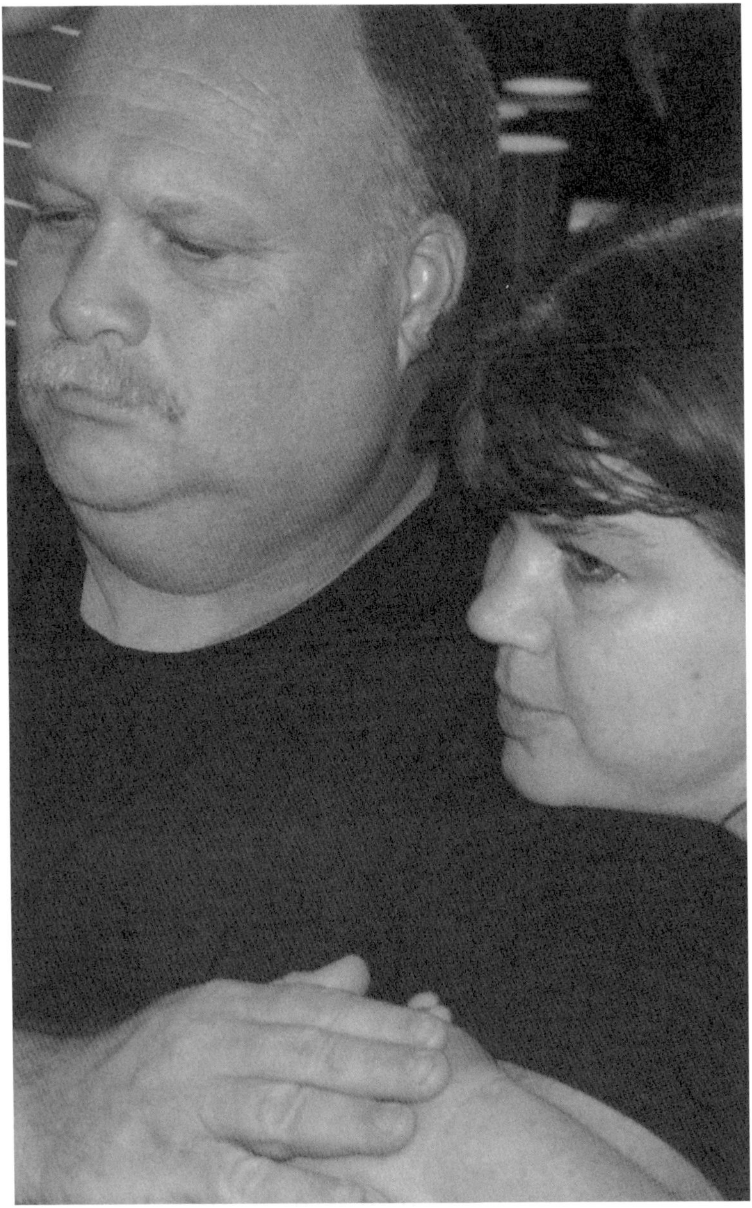

Day 27

She watches over the affairs of her household and does not eat the bread of idleness. Proverbs 31:27

The "bread of idleness" is an interesting phrase. Where does that come from? Is idleness like a poison that one can consume?

The slothful person is often pictured in the Book of Proverbs sitting or lying down and doing nothing: "How long will you lie there, you sluggard? When will you get up from your sleep?" (See Proverbs 6:6-11.) In an agrarian society, you have the daylight hours to do your work. You have the springtime to do your planting. You have a few weeks to bring in the harvest (Proverbs 10:4-5). Diligence and disciplined activity are essential for the health and well-being of the family and the village. When hard work and survival are so closely connected, it is easy to see why, as the apostle Paul stated, "If a man will not work, he shall not eat" (2 Thessalonians 3:10).

When I was a boy we leased a farm near Richland Springs, Texas. We grew peanuts, pecans, and pears, among other things. The pear harvest was overwhelming the first year we lived there. The trees were loaded, their branches bent to the ground. We harvested some of them, but we did not have a market for those pears. We canned what we could, and the rest spoiled in just a couple of weeks as they dropped to the ground and the birds and insects ate them full of holes. The agricultural harvest waits for no man. The farmer must plan for and be committed to long hours of labor when the fruit is ripe.

We have today. Yesterday is gone, and we should dismiss it from our minds. Tomorrow is not assured, and it could easily rain or turn cold. Today the sun is shining, I am strong and healthy, and I should be doing the things of first priority. Wisdom dictates that I care for my family first, that household affairs are in order, and that I do not fritter away my time while important matters go unattended.

Scripture Reading: Proverbs 27

Prayer: Lord Jesus, help me set aside the anxieties that paralyze me. Give me faith to walk through this day attending to the things that matter most. Keep me from wasteful activities that drain my spirit and are poor substitutes for worthy and honorable endeavors.

Day 28

Her children arise and call her blessed; her husband also, and he praises her. Proverbs 31:28

Our children are pretty hard on us, especially when they are young. As they age, they usually mellow in their criticism and may even be susceptible to some admiration of the parents that embarrassed them as teenagers.

I always loved my mother, but I did not always appreciate her. She always loved me, and she always thought I was a bundle of great potential. The role of the mother is to nurture toward independence the one she loves. The role of the child is to grow up enough to be grateful for the woman who brought him into the world.

These children have matured enough to see their mother's beauty and goodness. They know her more fully than she is known by her admiring friends and acquaintances. Sometimes when flattering adjectives are used for their mother, they roll their eyes and say softly, "Whatever." The woman others know from observation they know from the inside out. Others know her with her makeup in place and her garments perfectly starched and pressed. Her offspring know her with her hair hanging in wet strands standing in a bathrobe scrambling the eggs.

All makeup and public persona aside, these children admire their mother. She is blessed because she has blessed them. They have learned through their own journeys of difficulty what a magnificent woman she is. And they are not afraid to give her the praise she rightfully deserves.

Scripture Reading: Proverbs 28

Prayer: Dear Lord, thank you for the gift of life that you gave to me through my biological mother. Bless her today, wherever she may be, whatever she is doing. Help me today to be the kind of friend and parent who is called "blessed" by those who know me best.

Day 29

Many women do noble things, but you surpass them all. Proverbs 31:29

Virtue is never transient. It comes with a lifetime guarantee of integrity and faithfulness. Virtue is not a matter of doing a few things well. It is the development of an inner life that values most what matters most to God. Virtue shows itself externally, but it is a matter of the heart.

Many people—most people—do some good things in their lives. They give a generous donation to a worthy cause. They rescue a wounded animal. They provide dinner for a bereaved neighbor. These acts are intrinsically good, but they do not necessarily render the individual a person of virtue.

I have spent a lot of time in prisons ministering to those who have committed the most heinous crimes imaginable. Even on death row I have heard the self-righteous assertions of those who consider themselves better than others: they may have killed someone, but at least they are not pedophiles. With this warped morality, everyone can at least look down on someone.

Virtue is the ongoing determination to be faithful to the highest ideals, to strive toward the loftiest goals. The most virtuous among us do not make up their own moral hierarchy; they receive the hierarchy of values from God himself. In this way they avoid the worst form of egotistical self-righteousness: supposing that they are the source of "the knowledge of good and evil." We have all eaten that poisonous fruit, but we do not all have to live under the branches of that tree.

We achieve our greatest moral advance when we acknowledge our own incurable moral brokenness and reach out to receive the righteousness which comes from God alone, the righteousness that comes by grace through faith in the Lord Jesus. Embracing the righteousness that Jesus Christ bought for us on the cross when he died—that is the greatest act of moral transformation any human can undergo. It takes all pride and ego out of goodness. It strips us to our ugly essence then clothes us with the beautiful garments of forgiveness and mercy that Christ alone provides.

Scripture Reading: Proverbs 29

Prayer: Dear God, forgive me for the egocentric way I pass judgment. Deliver me from the seat of judgment and take me to the seat of mercy today. Give me the wisdom to live under mercy so that I may know myself and others more fully and may serve you more faithfully.

Day 30

Charm is deceptive, and beauty is fleeting; but a woman who fears the Lord is to be praised. Proverbs 31:30

Here is the one reference to God in the poem of the Virtuous Woman: she is a "woman who fears the Lord." This may strike us as a little strange that a person of virtue has been described in some detail in the Bible without any comment about her devotional life, her worship schedule, or her tithing commitment. What do we make of this? Is the love of God not a part of excellent living?

I think the this woman's love for God is described quite fully in Proverbs 31 based upon her practice of the Second Commandment, love of neighbor. She is described and defined by the nature of her visible connections to those around her. Paul declares that the keeping of the Second Commandment is the fulfillment of the law. He makes this assertion with no reference to the First Commandment, love God (see Romans 13:8-10).

The Book of Proverbs concludes its prologue (Proverbs 1:1-7) with a thematic summary: the fear of the Lord is the beginning of knowledge (Proverbs 1:7). This theme appears again and again in the proverbs that follow. And now it brings to a fitting conclusion the entire book by announcing that this amazing woman of virtue fears the Lord.

The fear of the Lord is both attitude and action. It is an attitude of submission to God's law and God's way. It is the action of keeping, of obeying, his commandments. Worship and obedience toward God are the first steps on the journey of wisdom. Wisdom begins and ends with this great truth.

After all, wisdom is not what we invent. It is what we discover on our way to worship and obey. We find wisdom in the being and activity of God himself. Other things fade and change. But the fear of the Lord is an unmoving constant for the inner you. It is the needle on our moral compass that, drawn to God's being, keeps us right and true.

Scripture Reading: Proverbs 30

Prayer: Father of lights, forgive me for giving greater value to physical beauty than I do to inner character. Forgive me for valuing material things above the eternal things. Keep me straight today so that I may fear you as I should and stay true to the life-giving ideals that flow from who you are.

Day 31

Give her the reward she has earned, and let her works bring her praise at the city gate. Proverbs 31:31

This woman is going to be praised. In fact, her children "arise and call her blessed; her husband also, and he praises her" (Proverbs 31:28). She should be praised, according to verse 30. And now we are told that "her works bring her praise at the city gate."

If only God is truly worthy of our praise, then why is this excellent but imperfect woman receiving praise? Is this really okay? It is inevitable for sure. The people who love her most and know her best—her husband and children—are singing her praises. And the work that she has done is bringing her honor in the city gate. That she cannot prevent. When someone lives life with excellence and virtue, people will speak highly of them. We will not stop that practice, and we should not.

If the woman were giving herself praise, that would be a problem. Proverbs 27:2 reads, "Let another praise you, and not your own mouth; someone else, and not your own lips." Nothing hangs so ugly on a human as self-glorification.

Praise is a very powerful thing. It motivates and challenges and blesses the soul. When we praise our children or grandchildren, we can see them brighten up and pull up straight and tall. That is natural whenever we are told that we have done well.

However, we should not do good in order to be praised. If we do that, Jesus said, we lose our eternal reward. Our actions become nothing more than a show. We are not expressing any goodness of heart when we are seeking the applause of others. We are only displaying our depraved and proud nature (see Matthew 6:5-8).

Our good works are likely to garner recognition. The Virtuous Woman who is the subject of this poem did not escape notice. Neither could Dorcas elude the praises of those she blessed in life or in death (see Acts 9). In fact, the accolades cast their way have reverberated through the generations since they walked this earth.

I want to add my praise to the thousands who have admired the person of excellence in Proverbs 31. And I want to do so in the finest way I know. Imitation, they say, is the sincerest form of flattery.

Scripture Reading: Proverbs 31

Prayer: Father in Heaven, you have challenged me with this portrait of a beautiful person. I feel inadequate as I read these verses, yet I know the strength of your grace in my life. I ask that today I might draw nearer to this amazing ideal of excellent character. Help me to imitate her in her excellence and so be more like you.